LINUX

Easy Linux For Beginners

Your Step-By-Step Guide to Learning
The Linux Operating System and
Command Line

Felix Alvaro

Acknowledgments

Firstly, I want to thank God for giving me the knowledge and inspiration to put this informative book together. I also want to thank my parents, my brothers and my partner Silvia for their support.

Table of Contents

Acknowledgments 2
Table of Contents 3
Introduction 5
Chapter One: Getting Started 7
Chapter Two: Understanding Linux 17
Chapter Three: Linux Installation 24
Chapter Four: Your First Linux Experience 35
Chapter Five: Post-Installation Activities 50
Chapter Six: Linux Applications 66
Chapter Seven: Using the Linux Command Line 72
Chapter Eight: Basic Administration and Security 78
Chapter Nine: Introduction to Scripting 92
Before You Go 98

© Copyright 2015 by D.A.Alvaro - All rights reserved.

This document is geared towards providing exact and reliable information in regards to the topic and issue covered.

It is not legal to reproduce, duplicate, or transmit any part of this document in either electronic means or in printed format. Recording of this publication is strictly prohibited.

The information provided herein is stated to be truthful and consistent. Under no circumstances will any legal responsibility or blame be held against the publisher for any reparation, damages, or monetary loss due to the information herein, either directly or indirectly.

Respective author owns all copyrights not held by the publisher.

The information herein is offered for informational purposes solely, and is universal as so. The presentation of the information is without contract or any type of guarantee assurance.

The trademarks that are used are without any consent, and the publication of the trademark is without permission or backing by the trademark owner. All trademarks and brands within this book are for clarifying purposes only and are the owned by the owners themselves, not affiliated with this document.

Introduction

Hi there! Congratulations on acquiring this book. You have made a great investment in the attainment of new knowledge in Linux.

My name is Felix Alvaro and I am an Internet Marketer, Entrepreneur and Author with the mission to motivate and inspire you to achieve your goals, by sharing my knowledge and experience through my books.

Because of your interest in this book, I am going to presume that you have heard about Linux. While it is not the most popular operating system used in most personal computers, Linux is definitely the most powerful. Here's a trivia: 98.8% of the world's fastest systems (think supercomputers) use the Linux kernel. If they are using it, then why shouldn't you?

Aside from personally using it on your own computer, the demand for Linux administrators has been characteristically high ever since big companies adopted the open-source operating system for their servers.

Regardless if you are getting this book to experience using Linux the first time or if you are eyeing to get Linux Professional certifications in the future, buying this book definitely puts you in the right track. I can promise that this book will equip you with the information that you need to get you started and keep you going in your Linux knowledge.

Getting started with Linux is easy once you become familiar with the system's features. In this guide, I am going to break everything down for you in a simple approach that will enable you to grasp everything quickly. I also don't assume you know something already and go into detail for every concept I teach.

In the first chapter I will be giving you an overview on Linux and also telling you why it is such an amazing Operating System to master.

Let's get to it!

P.S Don't forget to claim your FREE Bonus video course at the end of this book. Enjoy!

Chapter One: Getting Started

In this first chapter I will be giving you an overview on Linux and will be discussing the differences it has to other Operating Systems that make it one of the best Operating Systems out there.

What is an Operating System?

A computer, complete with all its parts – the CPU, mouse, monitor, and keyboard – will not work without a central program that will piece it all together. In order to use a PC, you need a piece of software inside which will take care of making the hardware work for you. A special kind of software which is between the hardware of the PC and the programs (Software as well) that you want to use and work with. This piece of software is the Operating System or more easily referred to as just OS.

In short, an operating system is the software that brings together a computer's hardware and the different programs that you want to install on it. Without it, when you boot up a PC you will not get anything on the monitor and neither mouse nor keyboard will work. You will be unable to watch videos, listen to music, edit photos, or to simply write a note.

With that said, an operating system is responsible for doing the following tasks:

- **Detect hardware** – An OS is responsible for validating the components of a computer during boot up (hard drive, CPU, network cards, mouse, etc.) and loading the corresponding drivers and modules for the hardware to properly run.
- **Manage processes** – Similar to the way our mind works, several processes or applications are running on a computer at the same time. It is the OS that is responsible for allocating CPU resources and share it among the processes. The OS also provides the user the option to start, stop, or restart a process.
- **Manage memory** – Each application needs a specific amount of RAM and swap memory to function. The OS is responsible for assigning memory allocations and for handling memory requests.
- **Initiate user interfaces** - An OS offers users ways to access the system either via a command line or a graphical user interface (GUI)
- **Establish file systems** – The OS handles the management of files (access, directories, and structure), including the access to the file system.
- **Manage access and user authentication** – An OS allows for creating user accounts with different permissions for access to files and processes.
- **Provide platform for administrative use** – A computer's OS provides a platform for the administrator to add users, allocate disk space, install

software, and to perform activities to manage the computer.
- **Start up services** – The OS manages several processes running in the background known as *daemon processes*.

Let's take it to a setting that we can all relate to – a manager at work. An OS is like a manager who keeps the different parts of the team in check, assigns tasks, distributes work load, and checks everyone's performance. While every member of a team has specific job responsibilities, a manager keeps the team working together cohesively.

Examples of an operating system that you have probably heard of are Windows 10 (and its predecessors), Mac OS X Yosemite (and the previous releases), and Unix.

So where does Linux fit in? We'll discuss it in the next section.

What is Linux?

Linux is an operating system, similar to the examples mentioned in the previous section, and is often described as Unix-like.

The stark difference between Linux and other operating systems lies in the fact that Linux is an open-source operating system. This means that Linux is continuously developed collaboratively and unlike Windows and OS X which are both tied to respective companies (Windows and Apple), not one company owns Linux' development and support. Building Linux is a shared vision, with different companies sharing researches, development, and the associated costs. This open source cooperation among companies and developers has led to making Linux one of the best ecosystems for use from small digital wristwatches to servers and supercomputers. Based from statistics, there are at least 100 companies and more than 1000 developers who work together for every kernel release.

Linux is composed of a *kernel*, the core control software, plus plenty of libraries and utilities that provide different features. Linux is available through many *distributions*. These are what we can call Linux flavours. Distributions are a group of specific kernels and programs. The most popular ones include Arch, SUSE, Ubuntu, and Red Hat. The book focuses on functions present on most Linux distributions although these distributions have their own specific tools at times.

This operating system was first used as a server OS and then was used as base for Android development. Up until now, Linux has the largest market share when it comes to server OS but one of the least popular for personal and home use such as desktops and laptop computers. In the next sections, we will go on an in-depth discussion of the reason why Linux is better compared to other operating systems.

In addition to the tasks performed by an operating system, Linux has the following characteristics:

- **Supports clustering** – Multiple Linux systems can be configured to appear as one system from the outside. Service can be configured among clusters and still offer a seamless user experience.
- **Runs virtualization** – Virtualization allows one computer to appear as several computers to users. Linux can be configured as a virtualization host – where you could run other OS such as Windows, Mac OS, or other Linux systems. All the virtualized systems appear as separate systems to the outside world.
- **Cloud Computing** – Linux can handle complex, large-scale virtualization needs – including virtual networks, networked storage, and virtual guests.
- **Options for Storage** – Data need not to be always stored in your computer's hard disk. Linux offers different local and networked storage options such as Fibre Channel and iSCSI.

I will not be discussing the functionalities mentioned above in detail because of its advanced applications. These, however, are things that are good to know when comparing Linux to other operating systems.

History of Linux

Linus Benedict Torvalds, a student from Finland, created Linux in 1991 using C and assembly language. Linux was developed as a free, open source, open license operating system, which enables developers around the world to study and modify the OS. Since the release of the initial source code in 1991, it has grown now to more than 18 million lines of code under GNU General Public License.

Initially, Torvalds named the operating system he invented as *Freax*, a combination of the words "free", "freak", and "x". He uploaded his files to an FTP server where his colleague, Ari Lemmke, was the FTP server administrator. Lemmke thought *Freax* was not a good sounding name so he renamed the folder to *Linux* without telling Torvalds. Later on, Torvalds approved the name change.

In 1992, Linux was licensed under GNU GPL and the first Linux distributions (also called *distro*) were created – Boot-root, MCC Interim Linux, Softlanding Linux System (SLS), and Yggdrasil Linux where one of the first few released in the same year. Several distributions have been created over time: Slackware - the oldest existing distro, Debian - the largest community distribution, and commercial distributions Red Hat and SUSE.

In recent years, Linux has seen more developments. The server market revenue of Linux has already exceeded that of

Unix. The Linux-based mobile OS Android has gained 75% of the market share. In 2015, Linux Kernel Version 4.0 was released.

Through collaborative works, Linux is now one of the most powerful operating systems. Data shows that 98.8% of the world's fastest systems use the Linux kernel. Isn't it comforting to know that you are using the same OS as these supercomputers?

Linux as Compared to other Operating Systems

Now, let's get to the important question: Is Linux better than the others? Let's compare Linux with other well-known operating systems.

- **Cost**

  If you obtained Windows legally, you would have paid more than $100 and even more for the Pro version. Linux, on the other hand, is free of charge. For Linux commercial distributions, companies sell services such as support and documentation but the OS itself comes for free.

- **Viruses**

  Linux hardly gets any viruses. Since most PCs run on Windows, attackers target Windows OS. The open-source policy of Linux is key. With many developers working on Linux, there are more eyes focused on seeing security flaws. There's plenty of help too, if ever a real Linux virus comes around. Proprietary operating systems are tied with the number of employed engineers and resources they have. With Linux, any developer from around the world can simply download the source code and help out in finding and solving flaws.

- **System Stability**

As mentioned in the previous section, Linux are used in servers and supercomputers. Large-scale systems can go on for years without restarting the server. The time when a proper restart is performed is during kernel upgrades – even upgrades for software running on a Linux server only perform a service restart and not a node restart.

Compare that to the number of times you've experienced losing data because the program crashed or the time when you plugged in a device and you saw the "Blue Screen of Death" in Windows. I am not saying that you will not turn off your computer when running on Linux, but the option is there, if you wish to.

- **Installation**

When you install Linux (any of its flavours – Ubuntu, Fedora, etc), you get all the stuff that you need – text editor, spreadsheet, presentation program, photo editor, web browser, movie player, PDF reader, and the likes. As compared to Windows and other OS, once you have the OS set-up, you will have to install all the other software that you need one-by-one.

It also holds true for hardware drivers too. In Windows, you would have to install the drivers first. Drivers usually come in CDs when you purchase hardware. Now, think about the time when you would need to install the driver and you couldn't find the CD for it? You would have to go to the manufacturer's website to download the specific driver. In Linux, drivers are included in the Linux Kernel installation – you get to save time and it's a lot more convenient.

- **Support**

    Linux has a large community online where new users can get information, read FAQs, and ask questions if there are programs or features that you think are not working right. The great thing about open-source is that with plenty of people involved in the OS, there are unlimited number of resources that you can use and learn from. All these come for free too!

These are some of the reasons why Linux is a better OS compared to others. However, do note that Linux uses open-source software so if you are concerned about any of the items listed below, then you should stick to Windows or your current OS:

- You need to work using proprietary software. If you absolutely cannot find an open source program that will match the proprietary software that you need, keep your current OS.
- You are a serious gamer. Majority of games are only made compatible with Windows.
- Hardware is not yet supported in Linux. Very new hardware like those released only in the few months might not yet be supported in Linux. Hardware vendors usually release drivers only for Windows and Mac since these are the most popular.

Most individuals with Linux installed do away with these by what is called *dual-booting*. This is the option of installing both Windows and Linux on your device so you can choose either of the OS depending on your needs.

***

In this chapter, we have discussed what Linux OS can do and how it compares with other existing operating systems. In the next chapter, we will go in depth and understand how a Linux operating system works.

Chapter Two: Understanding Linux

In this chapter, I will provide short information on this operating system's architecture and also discuss about the different flavours of Linux that a beginner can choose from.

Linux Architecture

Linux architecture can be divided into two: the User Space and the Kernel Space.

- **User Space** – This is where the applications are used. The GNU C library in the User space is the interface that connects to the kernel and transitions between User and Kernel space. This uses all the available memory.
- **Kernel Space** – All Kernel services are processed here. The Kernel space is further divided into 3.
    - **System Call Interface** – A User process can access Kernel space through a System Call. When a System Call is performed, arguments are passed from User to Kernel space. This is the layer that implements basic functions.
    - **Kernel Code** – This is the architecture-independent code and can be seen in all architectures that Linux supports.

- **Architecture-Dependent Kernel Code** – This is the layer for platform-specific codes.

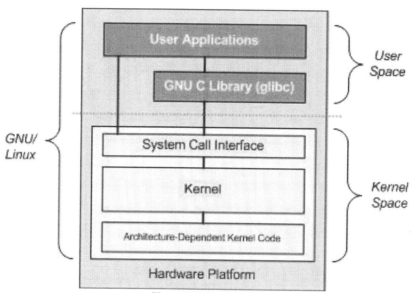

Figure 1: Linux Architecture

Linux Distributions

Each Linux distribution consists of a Linux kernel plus utilities and configuration files. Most Linux distributions can be downloaded from their websites.

Let's take a look at how several of the popular Linux distributions, or flavours, differ from each other based on the following criteria:

- **Availability**

    As previously mentioned, Linux is a free software but companies offering a support contract and proprietary components offer it for a fee. In the table below, Red Hat Enterprise and SUSE Enterprise both offer Linux commercially but they also have the free alternatives – Fedora and openSUSE.

- **Package Format**

    Linux distributions come in packages. Packages are files grouped into one single file. RPM is the most commonly used.

- **Release Cycle**

    This is how often a distribution releases new software. The ones with shorter release cycles provide the latest software in the shortest possible length of time while those distributions with longer release cycles aim to offer the most stable environments possible. A distribution can have it done both ways. Take a look at Ubuntu who releases both long-term support (LTS) versions (longer cycle) and the latest software through a 6month cycle.

Distribution	Availability	Package Format	Release Cycle
Arch	Free	pacman	Rolling
CentOS	Free	RPM	Approx. 2-yr
Debian	Free	Debian	2-yr
Fedora	Free	RPM	Approx. 6-mo
Gentoo	Free	ebuild	Rolling
Mint	Free	Debian	6-month
openSUSE	Free	RPM	8-month
Red Hat Enterprise	Commercial	RPM	Approx. 2-yr.
Scientific	Free	RPM	Approx. 6-mo
Slackware	Free	tarballs	Irregular
SUSE Enterprise	Commercial	RPM	2-3 years
Ubuntu	Free	Debian	6-month

Table 1: Comparison of Popular Linux Distributions

To help you decide on which is the right distribution for you, consider the criteria mentioned above and research on the other fields listed below:

- **Desktop environment**: Do your research and find out if the particular distribution that you're eyeing has a basic look and feel that you like plus check how customizable it is
- **Hardware Compatibility**: Depending on the hardware that you are using, some drivers might not be available yet by the time you install your distro. Check from online resources first to know which ones can be supported out-of-the-box.
- **Community Support**: Find the one with a large online community. The bigger the community is, the easier it will be to find documentation and get support.

I personally recommend Linux Mint for those who have never used Linux before. The installation is easy and fuss-free, plus the menus are familiar (see image below). It also comes with an added bonus of proprietary software that comes preinstalled (eg. Adobe Flash, MP3 support).

Figure 2: Mint Desktop

Once you are familiar with Mint and you feel like you want to branch out to other distributions, I recommend Ubuntu as your next distro. Ubuntu makes Linux easy to use for the experienced, average user. The distro also comes with a standard set of programs that can get you working in no time after installation.

Figure 3: Ubuntu Distribution

***

In this chapter, we talked about the different components that make up Linux and touched on the differences of popular distributions. I hope this will help you find the right distribution that you want to start your Linux experience on. In the next chapter, I will walk you through the process of Linux installation.

Chapter Three: Linux Installation

In this chapter, we will discuss about finally installing Linux in your computer. Depending on how you want your setup to be, you can either wipe your hard drive clean and replace your existing OS with Linux or keep your existing OS and share the disk with Linux. The latter will take a few more steps to do the hard disk partitioning.

Linux on Your PC

For beginners, there are two ways on how you can test the waters with Linux.

First, you can get a Linux Live CD. If you want to leave your current OS untouched but you want to try out Linux first, then this is the best option. Using a Live CD will allow you to boot from a CD/DVD or USB drive and use Linux. Once you're done, remove the CD/USB and reboot the computer to use your current OS. When you're running the Live CD, you might notice it to be a little slow since the OS is loading from the drive. You can get Live CDs from Knoppix http://knoppix.net/get.php or from Ubuntu http://www.ubuntu.com/download/desktop/try-ubuntu-before-you-install.

Second, you can directly proceed to installing Linux on your computer, either on its own or shared with your existing OS.

The steps discussed in the succeeding sections apply to both using Live CD and those installing Linux.

Pre-Installation Steps

Before proceeding with the installation, it will be a good idea to check your PC's hardware first. You may check the hardware vendor's site to check the compatibility list.

- **DVD Drive**: To install Linux, you must have a DVD drive and your computer must be able to boot from the drive. If your hard drive controller is IDE/ATA or USB DVD, this will work in Linux.
- **Hard Drives**: This is not necessary if you will be using the Live CD. If you will be installing Linux, it is ideal to have at least 4GB of disk space. Linux supports IDE and SCSI hard drive controllers.
- **Keyboard**: All keyboards work with Linux.
- **Monitor**: Most distribution installers can detect modern monitors. If you find that it does not display well, choose a monitor type and a specific resolution (1024x768).
- **Mouse**: PS/2 or USB mouse works with Linux.
- **Network Card**: Installers can detect most network cards. If you find that you are having

problems with one, find additional information online.
- **Processor**: Minimum processor speed required is 700 MHz. New processor speeds nowadays are way more than this value. In terms of speed, the higher the number, the better.
- **RAM**: The bigger RAM, the better. Minimum required is 512MB. Check the corresponding RAM for your specific distro – others might require a bigger RAM allocation.
- **Sound Card, Video Card, Printer**: Make sure that these are compatible with Linux. Refer to the hardware vendor's site for more information.

Next, make space for Linux.

If you opt to install Linux without removing your current OS, note that your existing operating system uses the whole hard drive. This means that Linux and your current OS needs to share the hard drive so that the two operating systems can co-exist. You will need to partition and divide the hard drive. If you choose to take this route, ***make sure to take a backup*** of your system because there is the risk of wiping out the data on the drive.

To facilitate partitioning, you can get hard drive partitioning products that runs on Windows or you can use a GUI called

QTParted that comes with most Linux distributions. Some distributions (like openSUSE or Xandros Desktop) can reduce Windows partition and automatically create partitions for Linux. In case your distribution of choice offers this feature, you will no longer need a partitioning tool.

Here are the partitioning steps for Ubuntu:

Once Ubuntu boots up and the GUI desktop appears, follow the following steps to reduce the size of the Windows partition:

1. Click on System➪Administration➪GParted from the Ubuntu desktop. The GParted window will appear, and will show the drives it finds on your PC. The first hard drive that you will see will have a device name /dev/sda, the next one will be named as as /dev/sdb, and so on.

2. On the right side of the GParted window, choose the hard drive from the list of devices.

3. Choose the partition you want to resize. You need to look for the largest partition.

4. Select Resize/Move from the GParted menu.

5. Indicate the new size for the partition and then click Resize/Move. Indicate a size such that will give you 4GB or more of free disk space after the partition.

6. Click Apply to begin the applying the changes that you made.

After you get the free space required on your hard drive for Linux, you may now start installing your choice of Linux distribution.

Installation Steps

Go to the Linux distribution site and download the distro file. The file that you downloaded will come with the installation steps. In this section, let's talk about the general installation steps for any Linux distribution.

Step 1: Prepare your CD/DVD installer or Live CD. Download a copy of the distribution you plan to install and burn it into a CD/DVD.

Step 2: Ensure that your PC can boot from CD/DVD drive. If in case your PC still boots from the hard drive when you have a CD/DVD in the drive, change your Boot Devices first. Go into BIOS and change the order of boot devices – choose CD/DVD drive as the first boot option.

You can do this by rebooting your PC and pressing a key (F2 or Del on most computers) to go into the Setup menu. Verify the key for your computer brand and model. Once you're done assigning CD/DVD drive as the first boot option, put the disk in the drive and reboot your computer.

Step 3: If you are using a Live CD, reboot your computer. The computer will then boot up and load the OS from your Live CD.

If you are installing Linux, step 3 is to partition your drive. One of the options for partitioning was described in the previous section.

Once you already have the partitions in place, boot your computer from the CD/DVD drive and proceed with the installation. While installation procedures vary depending on the distribution, these are usually easy and straightforward steps. Refer to the installation screens that come with the documentation and you should be done in an hour or two.

There will be a few configuration steps as part of the installation such as setting the date and time, language, and selecting the software packages to install.

Once the installation is done, reboot your computer.

Installation Troubleshooting

We all want a smooth-sailing installation but in case things don't go your way, here are some initial troubleshooting tips that you can check.

Installer fails to start X Window

X Window is the graphical user interface included in many Linux distributions. If in case the installer did not detect the video card or for any other reason that the installer fails to start X, you can opt to do text mode installation.

Refer to the table below for some of the different ways on how you can access the text mode installation screen.

Distribution	How to Access Text Mode Installation
Debian	Default is text mode
Fedora	Type in **text** when you see the **boot:** prompt
SUSE	Press F3 and use the arrow keys to select the Text-Mode option. Press Enter.
Ubuntu	Default is text mode
Xandros	Press on the Shift key while rebooting from the CD/DVD drive. Choose Rescue Console. Type **quick_install** when you see the **bash** prompt.

Table 2: How to Access Text-Mode during installation

Is your distro not in the list? Find out how you can start text-mode installation for your distribution online.

The text mode installation screen is similar to the installation screens in which you have to respond to the prompts to perform the installation. Once you are in text mode, read the prompts carefully and follow the instructions.

X is not working after installation

If you happen to see the GUI during the installation but after the first reboot you are confronted with a grey screen or a black screen with an X in the middle, here are some steps that you can use to troubleshoot.

1. Reboot the PC. Press Ctrl+Alt+Delete.

2. Once the PC is booting up, press the A key if the distribution uses GRUB (GR and Unified Bootloader). For LILO, skip this step. The GRUB boot loader will then display a command line for the Linux kernel and will ask you to add what you want.

3. For GRUB, type a space and then word **single**. Press Enter. If using LILO, type **Linux single** then press Enter. The Linux kernel will boot in a single-user mode with the following prompt:

sh-3.00#

Once you see this prompt, you can now start to configure X.

Depending on the distribution you are using, X uses a configuration file to setup your display card, monitor, and resolution. The problem sometimes happens when the X configuration from the Linux installer is not right.

Solve this problem by creating a working configuration file:

1. Type the following command:

```
X -configure
```

Once you enter this command, the X server will create a configuration file. You'll see the screen go blank and then display several messages.

2. Use *vi*, a text editor and edit the file ///etc/xorg.conf.new. Insert the line below after Section "Files": line

```
FontPath "unix/:7100"
```

When using Fedora, you also need to change /dev/mouse to /dev/input/mice.

3. Start the X font server by typing the command below:

```
xfs
```

4. Type the line below to start the new configuration file.

```
X -config ///etc/xorg.conf.new
```

Once you see the blank screen with an X cursor, the configuration file is working fine.

5. Use Ctrl+Alt+Backspace to stop the X server

6. Type the command below to copy the config file to the /etc/X11 directory:

```
cp ///etc/xorg.conf.new /etc/X11/xorg.conf
```

7. Type the word **reboot** or press Ctrl+Alt+Delete to reboot the computer.

The login screen should come up if the config file change went well.

Most, if not all, Linux distributions have a solid community online. If you encounter problems during the installation, search for the problem, describe it in detail, or use the actual error message as your search keyword. You will find the information that you need and if not, you can always post in the forums and the community will be ready to help.

Visit the following forums for more information:

Ubuntu: http://ubuntuforums.org/
Linux Mint: http://linuxmint.com/forum/
SUSE: https://forums.suse.com/forum.php
Debian: http://www.debianhelp.org/

***

In this chapter, we discussed about the Linux installation proper. Now that you have Linux in your PC, we'll do a walkthrough of your first Linux experience.

Chapter Four: Your First Linux Experience

Now that your Linux system is up and running on your computer, let's start exploring the system.

Turning on Your PC

Once you turn on your computer, the boot loader – either GRUB or LILO, will come up and display the names of the operating systems installed in the computer. Use the arrow keys to select which OS you would like to load. This is applicable for PCs with two OS installed. If Linux is the only OS on your computer, wait for a couple of seconds as the boot loader starts up Linux.

Once Linux boots, a graphical login screen will be shown. Note however that other distributions don't require login upon start up. Each Linux distribution uses the **root** username for administrator access. In order to avoid doing any accidental changes to your system when you use root, login to your system using a different account. Assigning the root password is part of the installation process. Make sure that you know and remember your system's root password.

Here is an example an Ubuntu desktop after logging in:

Figure 4: Ubuntu Desktop

The desktop that comes up is either KDE or GNOME. We will discuss more of these in the succeeding sections.

Getting To Know Shell

The GUI from KDE or GNOME provides the best way to explore Linux through icons, windows, and pointers. However, in the event that the GUI does not work (as we have seen in the section about Installation Troubleshooting), it's a plus if we know how to use the terminal. Typing commands in the terminal is usually faster than navigating and clicking too.

In your desktop, browse and find the icon that looks like a monitor. This is the icon for the terminal window. If you can't find the icon, explore the Main Menu and find the one with the label **Console** or **Terminal**.

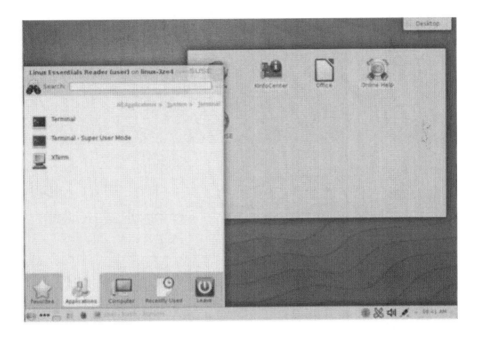

Figure 5: Terminal on a KDE Desktop

Here is how it looks like for Ubuntu:

Figure 6: Terminal Screen on Ubuntu

The shell is where you can run executable files and shell scripts. The shell is also what we call the *command line*. Commands are written using the general syntax below:

```
command option1 option2 . . . optionN
```

Here are a few sample commands that you can try in your Linux environment, with their corresponding output:

uptime

```
19:26  up 29 days,  1:39, 2 users, load
averages: 1.32 1.36 1.34
```

uptime is the command that shows the duration that the computer has been up. In this case, the computer has been up for the last 29 days or almost 1 month.

```
uname -srv
```
```
Linux 3.9.31.5-127.fc12.i686 #1 SMP Mon Nov
18 18:21:25 EST 2015
```

uname is the command to show the operating system name. *–s* (print the operating system name), *-r* (print the operating system release), and *–v* (print the operating system version) are options that you can use for the uname command. In the particular example, we want to use all three so we put n *–srv* to simplify. If we want to display the results as if we used all the options, we can use the *-a* option.

To know about the options that you can use for a particular command, you can use the *man* command.

```
man uname
```

The *man* command is extremely useful especially for beginners. This displays all the options that you can use. Try to use the command for every Linux command that you encounter.

To switch to *root* while in the shell, enter the command *su* - and then input your root password. Changing to root password while in the shell environment will allow you to run tasks that only administrators and superusers can do.

Linux Desktops

There are two commonly used GUIs that come with Linux distributions: GNOME and KDE. You can have both installed in your computer and switch between the two whenever you want to. Both GUIs also run on Unix, and while there are other GUIs that can be installed on Linux, these two remain as the most popular in use.

Here is a chart that compares both desktops:

Criteria	GNOME	KDE
Availability	Free	Free
Minimum System Requirements	700 Mhz CPU, 768 MB RAM	1 Ghz CPU, 615 MB RAM
Development Priorities	Focuses on freedom, accessibility, and developer-friendliness	Provides an aesthetically pleasing website with great configurability
Customization Experience	Interface is simple to use and great for first-time Linux users, advanced users may find its customization settings as limiting	Allow for versatile configuration that creates great looking desktop, but user has to learn to navigate the options. Customization makes it more resource-intensive
Default appearance (Note that both offers customization options)	Default setting: Toolbar at the top and a dock that pops out featuring	Default setting: toolbar at the bottom and a main menu.

	application icons	
Universal Search	Uses text-based search functionality	Uses text-based and menu-based navigation
Resource Usage and User Experience	Less resource-intensive than KDE	Good for users who came from Windows OS

Table 3: Comparison of GNOME and KDE desktops

Those are only some of the criteria in which the two GUIs differ. However, I encourage you to try both desktops so you can evaluate which one suits you best.

I'll show you some screenshots displaying the default settings of the desktops. GNOME desktop is shown in the next figure with its toolbar at the top that features details such as Applications Running, Day and Time, Volume, Network, and Battery Life.

Figure 7: A GNOME desktop running on Fedora

Figure 8: Gnome Folder Menu

The next set of screenshots show the default desktop for KDE. You'll find the panel at the bottom of the screen – similar to a Windows desktop.

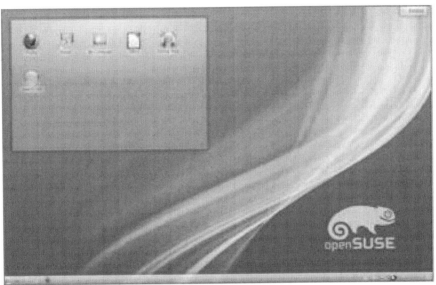

Figure 9: KDE Desktop on openSUSE

Figure 10: Menu Options on a KDE

Both can be customized to get the look and feel that you want to achieve. Go ahead and experiment with the desktops! Some distro only have one pre-installed but you can always get and install both. You can switch between the two in seconds.

Navigating the Linux Filesystem

Linux organizes files using a hierarchical system. Files are stored inside directories and these directories can also contain other directories. When you compare the Linux filesystem to Windows, you will find that there are no drive letters in Linux. All files are stored in a single root directory noted as / regardless of where the data is physically stored (hard drive, external drive, or CR-ROM).

To find a file in Linux, you also need the information about the directory hierarchy known as the pathname. The figure below dissects a sample path name.

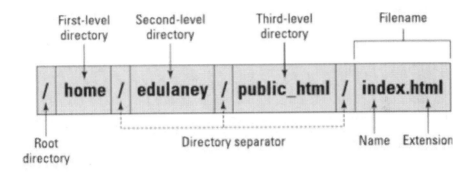

Figure 11: Pathname in Linux

The pathname is composed of a top-level directory, a directory hierarchy, and the filename with the file extension. All are separated by a forward slash (/).

Here is a listing of Linux top-level directories and the data that they contain:

Top-Level Directory	Files that the directory contains

/	Single root directory – file system base
/bin	Executable files such as Linux commands `cat,cp,ls`
/boot	Files that the boot loaders accesses during startup – including the Linux kernel
/dev	Files for the different hardware/devices
/etc	Initialization scripts and system config files
/home	User directories
/lib	Library files which includes driver modules
/lost+found	For lost files
/media	Mounting removal media filesystems
/mnt	Temporary directory for mounted filesystems
/opt	For storing application packages
/proc	Information on Linux processes
/root	Root user home directory
/sbin	Executable files for commands used by root user
/srv	For services hosted by the system (eg. FTP, web)
/tmp	Temporary directory – deleted during system reboot
/usr	Contains subdirectories for program files
/var	Log files

Table 4: Linux Top-level Directories

To navigate in the directories of Linux, you can either use the GUI to find a certain file by going through the folders, using the universal text-based search function, or by using the command line.

You can use the following useful commands in your terminal to navigate and work in the file system:

Commands	What it does
ls	List down all the contents of a director
cd /bin/	Changes directory and goes to bin dir
cd ~	the tilde (~) sign signifies the user's home dir – change dir to home director
cd ..	Means to change directory one level up. For example, you are currently /home/edulaney/, using the command will take you to /home/
mkdir	Command used to create directories
pwd	Short for present working directory. This command will display the directory where you are currently in.

Table 5: Directory Navigation Commands

Here I'll give out more commands that you can use to manage your files using the command line. Try this out on your terminal.

Commands	What it does
cat /home/edulaney/files/file1.txt	Command to print all the contents of file1.text in the screen
cp /home/ /tmp/	Copy contents of /home/ to /tmp
mv /home/edulaney/files/file1.txt /tmp/	Move the file file1.txt to the /tmp/ directory. You can also use this command to move the

47

	entire directory to another directory
rm *file1.txt*	Delete the file file1.txt. Take extra precaution in using the rm command especially when you are logged in as root.
find / -*name "linux*"*	The find command is a powerful tool that you can use when searching using the command line. The command here will search for any file or directory with a name that starts with *linux*

Table 6: Basic Commands for Managing Files

Explore more of the commands by using the *man* command.

Shutting Down your PC

Turning off your Linux PC is similar to how you do it in other operating systems. Click on the Main Menu, select Shutdown, and click on OK. This will initiate a system shutdown. Some distributions will not allow you to shut down the system without logging out first. To do this, click on Log Out and then select Shutdown in the login page.

***

Now that you are acquainted with the look and feel of a Linux environment, let's get to the post-installation activities such as managing your computer's hardware and installing applications.

Chapter Five: Post-Installation Activities

In this chapter, we will talk about the things that you can do after having your Linux OS installed – from managing hardware to installing additional software.

Managing Hardware and Peripherals

CPU

The operating system keeps programs and hardware working together smoothly. The capabilities of Linux are affected by the limitations of your system's hardware (for example, disk space and memory) so it is important to know more details about your computer's hardware.

Let's start with the CPU. The CPU performs all the computing and its speed (in MHz) signifies how fast your computer can handle transactions. Your CPU specs will tell also tell you about the CPU family (most common are x86 and x86-64) and the number of cores that it has. To know more about your CPU, use the Linux commands below:

Commands	What it does
uname -a	This command displays information about the

		machine, the processor architecture, and the operating system details. Using the *-p* option will show you the machine processor name. An example is *i386* or *x86_64 AMD Phenom (tm) II X3 700e Processor*
| lscpu | | This command returns more information about the system such as the number of CPUs and the CPU speed.<br><br>Sample output:<br><br>```
Architecture:          i686
CPU op-mode(s):        32-bit
Byte Order:            Little Endian
CPU(s):                4
On-line CPU(s) list:   0,1,2,3
Thread(s) per core:    4
Core(s) per socket:    2
Socket(s):             2
Vendor ID:             Intel
CPU family:            15
Model:                 3
Stepping:              4
CPU MHz:               2800
BogoMIPS:              5600.27
``` |
| cat /proc/cpuinfo | | This is a file that contains more information than the one displayed using the *lscpu* command.<br><br>Snippet from a */proc/cpuinfo* file:<br><br>```
processor: 1
vendor_id: Intel
cpu family: 11
model : 2
model name: Intel(R) Pentium(R) 4 CPU 2.86GHz
stepping: 4
microcode: 0xe
``` |

Table 7: Commands to get CPU information

Hard Disk

Next, let's discuss your computer's hard disk. In the installation chapter, I spoke about the importance of making sure that your computer has enough disk space for Linux and the possible need for partitioning your hard disk if you want to run two operating systems at the same time.

If you plan on adding a new disk in the future, learning how to partition will come in handy. Linux supports the following partitioning tools:

Fdisk Tools – This is composed of the text-based tools: *fdisk, cfdisk,* and *sfdisk.* These tools are great for use in partitioning, however, it could be a bit overwhelming for beginners who are not yet familiar with partitioning.

libparted Tools – The *libparted* library presents both GUI and text-based partitioning tools. One particular example is GParted as shown in the screenshot below. The interface makes it easier to use for beginners.

GPT fdisk Tools – These are tools created for GPT (Globally Unique Identifier Partition Table) disks using the *fdisk* tools.

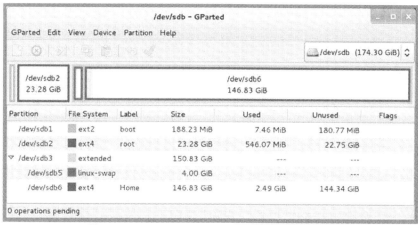

Figure 12: GParted - GUI-based partitioning tool

Here are some commands that you can use to check the existing disk space in your computer:

Commands	What it does
df -h	This command displays the disk space usage in all of the mounted devices. The *-h* option presents the results in a human-readable output, using G for gigabytes or M for megabytes sizes.
du */home/edulaney/files/*	This command displays all the files inside the specified directory and their corresponding file sizes. You can also specify a filename.
du -s */home/edulaney/files/*	The *–s* option provides the total file size of the specified directory

Table 8: Commands for Checking Disk Space

Removable Storage

Using storage such as USB flash drives and external hard disks in Linux works similarly when using Windows or Mac OS. Plug the device in and Linux will detect the device. Aside from accessing the drive via the desktop GUI, you can also navigate to the */media* directory and find the mounted subdirectory.

After you use the removable media, unmount the disk before removing it to avoid any disk issues. You can generally right-click on the Device Name and click on any of the options such as *Unmount*, *Eject Volume*, or *Safely Remove*.

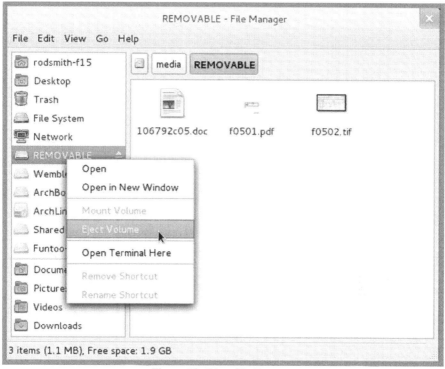

Figure 13: Eject Media

USB Devices

You can connect other devices such as human-interface devices (keyboard, mouse), cameras, mobile phones, scanners and printers to your Linux computer and expect that these work in a plug-and-play manner.

For printers, you will also need to set up the printer configuration after Linux detects the device. Follow the steps below to set-up a new printer. Note that the screenshots are taken from an Ubuntu distribution but this is similar to majority of the distros.

1. Click on **System Settings** then **Printers** in the desktop. Provide the root password.

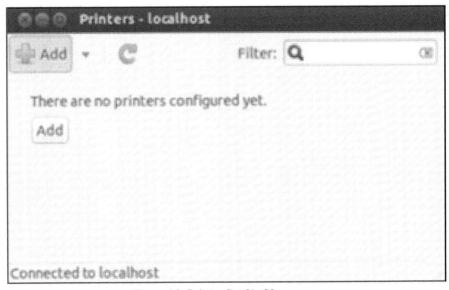

Figure 14: Printer Set-Up Menu

2. Click on the **Add** button. If the system has detected your printer, the device will show in the list. Otherwise, you will need to continue with the configuration and provide the printer drivers. Click **Forward**.

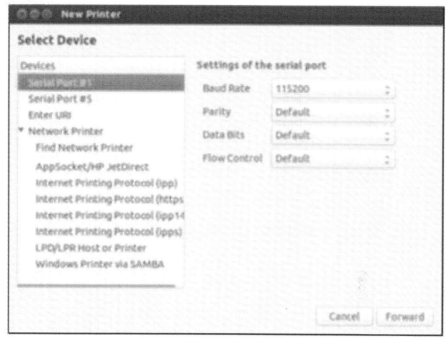

Figure 15: New Printer

3. Choose the correct driver. A list of available drivers will be shown – choose the one that is applicable for your printer make. If you do not find the driver on the list, you can also provide the printer driver or download the file online.

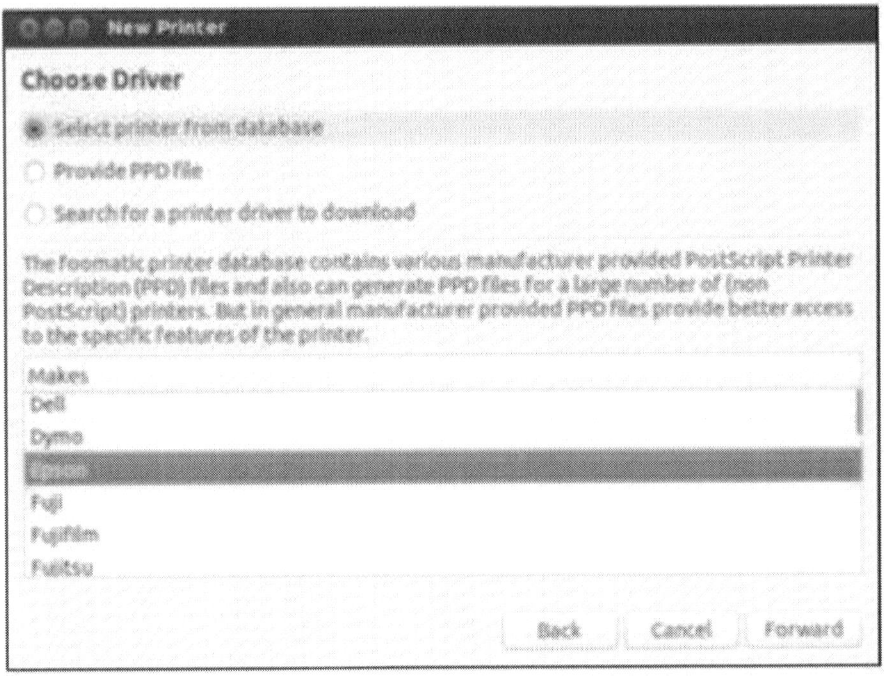

Figure 16: Selecting the Driver

4. Fill-up the printer name and description.

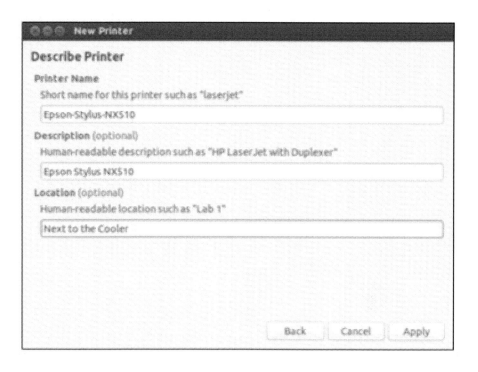

Figure 17: Printer Description

5. Lastly, print a test page to make sure it's working.

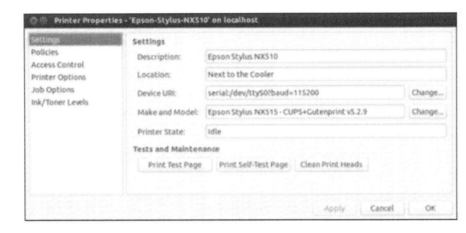

Figure 18: Printing a Test Page

Installing Additional Software

Linux-compatible softwares come in *.rpm* for RPM (Fedore, SUSE) or *.deb* for Debian (Debian, Ubuntu, Xandros) packages. Even if the type of packages varies, both RPM and Debian packages can be installed in any type of Linux distribution. Popularly used distributions provide a GUI for installing additional applications. In this section, I will discuss on the ways of installing software in Ubuntu and Fedora.

Installing Applications in Ubuntu

Debian-based distros use APT or the Advanced Packaging Tool.

You can use the command below to install packages to your computer.

```
apt-get install package-name
```

This command will download the specific package name that you want to install. In case you do not know the package name, you can search for a keyword.

```
apt-cache search keyword
```

For example, I am looking for an application that I can use to take screenshots in my GNOME desktop. I can further refine my search functionality with the following command:

```
apt-cache search screenshot | grep GNOME
```

The command will display the applicable lines that fit the search string:

```
shutter - feature-rich screenshot program
```

Shutter is the package name. Use the package name and run the `apt-get install` command again.

Aside from installing packages via the command line, you can also use the Software & Updates Tool. The GUI provides a simple and easy way to update your Ubuntu software and download packages.

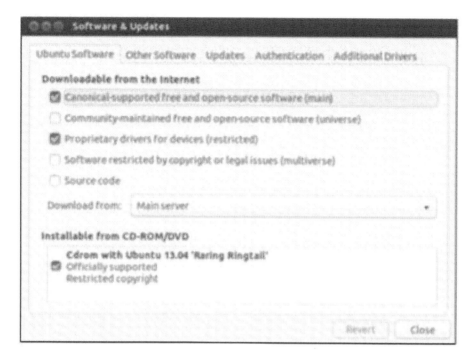

Figure 19: Software & Update Tool

Similar to Windows and Mac OS application stores, Ubuntu also has its Software Center where you can get new software and download the latest updates.

Figure 20: Ubuntu Software Centre

Installing Applications in Fedora

Fedora uses RPM packages. If you are using a GNOME desktop, you can simply use the ***Add or Remove Software*** tool (similar to Windows) to install new software.

Click on System➪Administration then on Add/Remove Software to access the menu. The utility will then display the Package Manager box showing the list of all packages. Select the corresponding check box and click on **Apply** or **Update** (if you are updating the packages). Clicking on the **Apply** button will install (or uninstall) the specific packages.

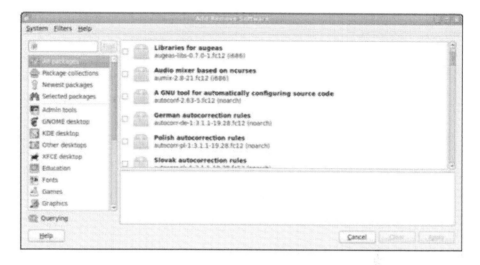

Figure 21: Fedora Add/Remove Packages

***

In this chapter, we reviewed the hardware setup and software installation steps that you can do post-Linux installation. For more detailed procedures, refer to the steps for the particular distribution that you are using. In the next chapter, we will briefly discuss the default Linux applications.

Chapter Six: Linux Applications

Linux distributions come pre-installed with applications for your computing needs. In this chapter, we will take a quick look at some of these applications.

Office Applications

Libre-Offfice suite is Linux's answer to Windows Office tools. The suite comes with a word processor, presentation application, spreadsheet, calendar, and calculator applications. If you are a Windows user, you might need sometime to get use to the interface but after a few times of using the apps, you'll eventually be familiar with it.

LibreOffice comes with the following applications:

- Writer – word processor. Files are created with a *.odt* file extension. Documents written with Microsoft Word are compatible with Writer.

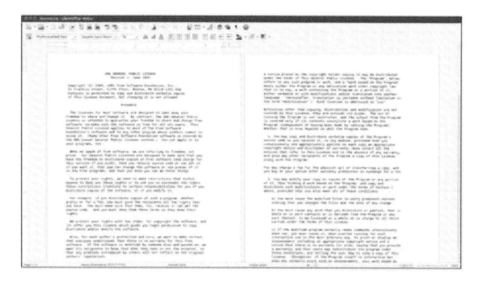

Figure 22: How Writer Looks Like

- Calc – spreadsheet program that works similarly to Microsoft Excel. Default file has .*ods* file extension

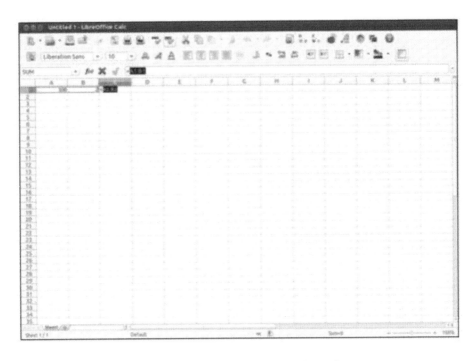

Figure 23: Calc Looking Like Microsoft Excel

- Impress – the counterpart of Microsoft PowerPoint. In Impress, you can make slide presentations based from existing templates or you can also customize the same way that you can do in Microsoft Office.

Figure 24: Made to Impress

All Libre-Office applications can be accessed from the Office option in the Main Menu.

Multimedia Applications

How about accessing multimedia? Linux distributions come with apps that allow you to open photos, listen to audio files, play videos, and burn CDs or DVDs.

SUSE and Xandros distributions are pre-installed with digiKam, a digital camera software. You also have the option to access your photos as files from a USB drive. Simply click on the storage drive name and view the photos.

Both KDE and GNOME come with an audio CD player. Put your CD in and the default audio player will detect and play the audio. For other sound files like MP3s, you can use players such as XMMS or Rhythmbox. Depending on the distro that you are using, you can go to the *Music Player application*, *Multimedia* or *Sound & Video* category to open the players.

In recent times, different distributions have already released a built-in CD/DVD burner functionality in their file managers. These work well but if you still want a separate application to burn files, you can use the most commonly used burn software such K3b for KDE.

Imaging Applications

Linux also makes sure that you get the photo editing and graphics creation applications that you need. The two most popular in the Linux world is The GIMP (GNU Image Manipulation Program) and GNOME Ghostview (GGv).

The GIMP is the equivalent of Adobe Photoshop. Users can perform image manipulation, composition, and creation. If you cannot find GIMP in the Graphics category from the main menu, check if you need to install the package first. Refer to the steps in the section Installing Additional Software (on page 40) to download and install The GIMP package. The application can read most image formats: JPEG, TIFF, PNG, PCX, and GIF. For more information about The GIMP, visit their website at at www.gimp.org

GNOME Ghostview can read PostScript or PDF documents and has similar functionalities as Acrobat Reader. To open Ghostview on a Fedora computer, click on Graphics then PostScript Viewer.

Explore the pre-installed applications and gauge if these suits your needs. Remember, there are plenty of Linux applications that you can use so go ahead and find out the best one for you.

***

In this chapter, we briefly discussed the different office, multimedia, and imaging applications that come with a Linux distribution installation. In the next chapter, we will establish a deeper understanding of the Linux command line.

Chapter Seven: Using the Linux Command Line

In Chapter Four, we discussed about the Linux Command Line or the *terminal* and how you can access it from your desktop. In the previous chapters, you were also able to use simple commands on the terminal. Each GUI action has a command-line equivalent. In this chapter, we will talk more about the different commands that you can use in Linux and also study the different shell features.

Using the Shell Features

You have now seen the capabilities of using the Bash shell. Performing tasks on the command line take lesser time than doing it in the GUI. To further enjoy the convenience of using the CLI (command line interface), here are some shell features that you should use:

- **Command Completion**

    Launch a terminal and try typing an unfinished command.

    For example, type the word below and press the **Tab** key.

```
unam
```

Notice that Linux will automatically complete the word to form uname. Next, remove the rest of the letters and just leave the letter u, Linux will then display all the list of commands that start with the letter 'u'. This feature makes it even faster for a user to type commands. You can even do this for filenames or directory names too. Type the first few letters of the filename and Linux will do the rest for you.

This is also helpful when you are trying to remember a command since Linux will list out all the commands starting with the letters that you put in. Combine this functionality with *man* and you should be able to locate the command that you are looking for.

- **Command History**

Linux makes it easier for users too with the command history feature. The system remembers commands you have recently typed in so you no longer need to retype. Simply use the arrow keys to view previous commands.

Here are some of the techniques that you can use to make the most out of this feature:

Keys to Use	What it does

Arrow Up/Down	Display the previous commands from the more recent going to the oldest entered
Arrow Right/Left	Moves the cursor one character to the right/left
CTRL key + A	Transfers cursor to the beginning of the line
CTRL key + E	Transfers cursor to the end of the line
Delete key	The character under the cursor is deleted
Backspace	The character to the left of the cursor is removed
CTRL key + R	Search for a particular command from the command history. After you use CTRL key + R, type the first few letters of the command that you want to use

Table 9: Command Line History Shortcuts

System administrators make good use of these features because it makes admin tasks easier and faster to complete. Try the techniques on some of the commands you've learned and see how cool it is to work using the command line.

Essential Linux Commands

As a new Linux enthusiast, you can perform many of the tasks using the GUI. However, if you do fancy learning more commands that you can use in the shell prompt, here's a cheat sheet of the most important Linux commands.

Command	What it Does
Help Commands	
info	Shows online information about a command
man	Shows details of a command
whatis	Shows a short description of a specific keyword
type	Shows the location of a command file
alias	Assign a command alias – especially useful for long commands
unalias	Remove command alias
Managing Files and Directories	
cd	Change directory
pwd	Displays the current directory
ln	Create links to files and directories
touch	To trigger a file stamp update for a file
Finding Files	
find	Search for a file based on name
whereis	Search for executable files
which	Search for files in the directories part of the PATH variable
Processing Files	
dd	Copy lines of data
diff	Display the results of comparing two files
more	Show a text file one page at a time – display can only go forward
less	Show a text file one page at a time – display can only go forward and backwards

75

wc	Display the count of the number of characters, words, and lines in a file
cat	Show a text file in one output
cut	Get sections of text in a file
grep	Display results of finding expressions in a file
sed	Perform editing commands then copy to a standard output
split	Specify a size to break a file into
sort	Arrange the lines in a file
uniq	Keep unique lines in a file and delete duplicates
Compressing a File	
compress	Use to compress a file
uncompress	If a file was compressed with a *compress* command, use this to decompress
gunzip	Use GNU Zip to decompress files
gzip	Compress files with GNU Zip
tar	Archive files with one or more directories
Date and Time	
cal	Show the calendar for the specified month or year
date	Show/Set the current date and time
Managing Processes	
bg	Run a program or a process in the background
free	Check for the free memory
kill	Stop a process
nice	Run a program with a low priority
ps	Show current running processes
top	Show list of CPU and memory utilization of processes
reboot	Restart the computer
shutdown	Turn off computer

Table 10: List of Important Linux Commands

Now, try out the commands above. If you are unsure of how to use the options for the commands, use the help commands (especially *man* and *info*) to find out more.

***

In this chapter, I gave you a list of commands and techniques that you can try in the command line. Continue on practicing with these commands and to research more online. In the succeeding chapter, we will learn about securing your operating system.

Chapter Eight: Basic Administration and Security

Your system is up and running now and the next thing you should think about is securing it. System administrators consider two aspects of security– host security and network security. If multiple users are using a computer, user directories and files should be secured and should not be accessed by any unauthorized person. Since your computer is connected to the internet, you have to protect it from access over the internet too. Let's discuss about these in the next sections.

Basic System Administration

Similar to popular operating systems like Windows and Mac OS, Linux distributions also come with GUI tools that can be used for performing administrative tasks. Adding and removing user accounts, performing software upgrades, managing hardware, installing new applications, maintaining the system's performance, and setting up and monitoring security are some of the activities that an administrator executes.

Figure 25: SUSE YaST for Administrative Tasks

The administrative tasks mentioned above can be performed using the YaST Tool when using SUSE. These functionalities are also available in Ubuntu and Fedora distributions.

Figure 26: Settings Screen for Ubuntu

Figure 27: Settings Screen for Fedora

Monitoring System Performance

To effectively monitor your computer's performance, the following aspects should be checked:

- **CPU and Memory Usage**

To see the processes that are consuming the most CPU resource and memory allocation, use the *top* command. This command displays the CPU load and used memory averages, the process IDs, the percentage of CPU used by the process, and the percentage of the memory used. The *top* command results are refreshed every 5 seconds. To exit the *top* command output display, press Q.

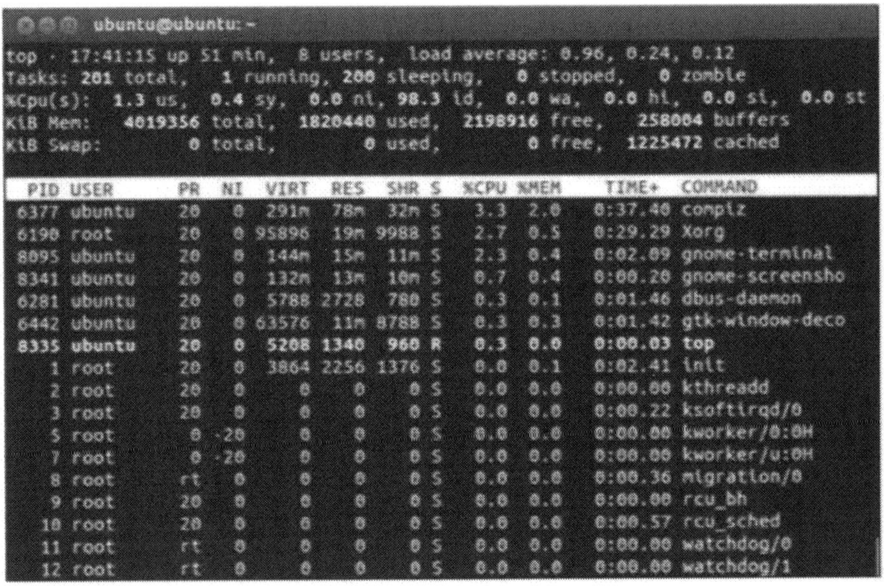

Figure 28: top command

To get a snapshot of the system status at the time the command was issued, use *uptime*. This command prints the load average for the last one, five, and fifteen minutes.

- **Hard disk space**

    Monitor the hard disk space to ensure that there is enough space for the system to perform tasks such as logging and backups. Use the *df -h* command to validate the disk space.

    Here's a sample output:

    ```
    Filesystem Size      Used Avail Use
    %        Mounted on
             /dev/hda1   7.1G 3.9G   2.9G
    59%  /
             /dev/hda2   99M  18M    77M
    19%  /boot
    ```

In the monitoring, set specific thresholds at which you, as the administrator will take an action. For example, once the used disk space percentage reaches a certain threshold like 80%, do a file cleanup to free up disk space. If the CPU reaches the allowed threshold, investigate which processes are using up the resources and do the necessary action (eg. wait for a process to finish, kill a process, etc). This is similar to killing processes in windows using the Task Manager.

User Management

Linux automatically creates multiple user accounts upon installation, even if you are the only one using your computer. The system uses these accounts for running programs. Different accounts safeguard the system, including files and directories, from unauthorized access. Users can be assigned to groups for easier facilitation.

To add, modify, or delete a user or group account, you can either use the GUI or do it via the command line. As a beginner, it would be good for you to try out both so you can see which one is the best method for you.

Managing Users and Groups Via GUI

Open YaST if you are using SUSE or the equivalent Settings Menu in your distribution. Click on the *Security and Users* or any similar User Management category.

Figure 29: YaST Add User

Click on the *Add* user button and supply the necessary information such as the user's full name, preferred username, and password. You can explore and configure additional information such as login attempt limit, password settings, and user groups. Once done, click on the OK button to continue creating the user account.

You can also modify or delete an account using the GUI. Perform the necessary account modifications and click on the OK button to proceed with the changes.

To create, modify, or delete a group, select *Groups* instead of users. The photo below shows the YaST screen for adding a new group. Provide the necessary information and click on the OK button to finish creating the group.

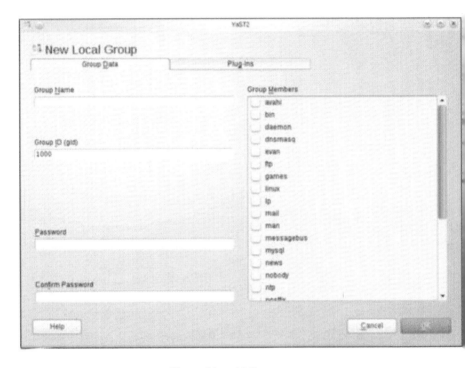

Figure 30: Add Group

Managing Users and Groups via CLI

Adding a new user via CLI consist only of a few lines of command. First, login as root by using the command su -

Use the command below to create a new account:

```
/usr/sbin/useradd -c "Kevin Jones" kjones
```

Next, set the password. Once you issue the command below, you will be prompted twice to enter and confirm the password.

```
passwd kjones
```

To modify an account, use the `usermod` command paired with the option that pertains to the information that you want to modify. To delete the user account, use the `/usr/sbin/userdel` *username* command.

To add a user group, you need to use the command `groupadd` *groupname*

For example, let's create a group named *office*. To create this group, enter the command below.

```
groupadd office
```

Since Kevin is a colleague at work, we will add him to the *office* group. To do this, use the command below:

```
usermod -G office kjones
```

To delete the group, use the command `groupdel office`

Again, I encourage you to use the *man* command to know more about the options that can be used for a specific command.

File Ownership

A user and group account owns a Linux file or directory. To see the owner of a particular file, use the command `ls -l` *filename*

Here is a sample output of the command. Choose a filename and try it on your terminal too!

```
-rw-rw-r-- 1 kjones office 40909 Jul 16 20:37 file1.txt
```

The first set of letters stands for the permission settings (execute, read, write). The second part with the value of *kjones office* signifies the user account and the group account that owns the file.

In case you want to change the ownership of the file from `kjones` to another user `rbentley`, login as root and use the command below:

chown *rbentley file1.txt*

Also, to change the group owner of the file, input the command:

chgrp *staff file1.txt*

Basic Security in Linux

Setting-up Passwords

When creating an account, make it a point as an administrator to create good passwords that are difficult to crack.

Remember to stay away from passwords formed from personal information (such as birthdays, street address, or names), single words that can be found in the dictionary, and simple combinations of alphanumeric numbers.

Use a password that contains mixed case (upper and lower case letters), has numbers or punctuations, or is written in reverse order. Also implement other preventive mechanism such as prompting the user to change his password every X number of days and to lock an account after Y number of login attempts.

Files Protection

To protect files from unauthorized access (view and modify), revisit your file permissions setting. In the preceding section, we talked about assigning the user and group owner for a file. Next, we need to specify the correct file permissions for the owner, the group, and global (all other users).

Let's go back to the result of an ls command:

```
rw-rw-r-- 1 kjones office 40909 Jul 16 20:37 file1.txt
```

The first set of letters (in green) signifies the file permissions for the user. The next set (in blue) is for the group, while the section in orange stands for the global permission.

- r – permitted to read the file contents
- w – permitted to write on the file

- x – permitted to execute (if the file contains a bash script)

This means that kjones has read and write permissions to the file. This is the same permission as the office group account. All other users (global) will only be allowed to read the file.

To change permissions, use the octal representation of the permission and specify the value for the 3 levels (user, group, and global).

Permission	Representation
rwx	7
rw-	6
r--	4
r-x	5
--x	1

Table 11: Permission Values

Let's now try to remove the write access from the group.

```
chmod 644 file1.txt
```

When you list the details for file1.txt again, the write access for the group should be already removed.

```
rw-r--r-- 1 kjones office 40909 Jul 16 20:37 file1.txt
```

There are several ways to secure your system such as setting up firewalls, securing internet services, and encrypting files, and using digital certificates. For the purposes of this book (Linux for Beginners), I only discussed the basic and initial security practices.

In the next chapter, I will give an overview about scripting, which is another aspect that you can practice in if you want to learn more about Linux.

Chapter Nine: Introduction to Scripting

We have come to the last chapter of the book. By this time, you are already familiar with how a Linux environment works and you must have already noticed how different it is from your previous OS. My suggestion to you is to take the experience a notch higher and start to learn how to create scripts in Linux. In this chapter, I will give a quick preview of scripting in Linux.

Choosing A Text Editor

Shell scripts are text-based files. To start your scripting journey, choose a text editor that works best for you. Linux distributions come with pre-installed text editors but the most commonly used ones are listed below:

- **vi** – Usually installed by default. Preferred by administrators because it is a powerful editor that is small in size and flexible.
- **emacs** – contains a lot of features but is not beginner-friendly
- **pico** – simplified version of *emacs* (without the features)
- **nano** – a clone of *pico* but comes with features

Download the packages for these editors and experience using it yourself. I personally use vi because of its ease in use, simplicity, and my overall comfort and familiarity with it.

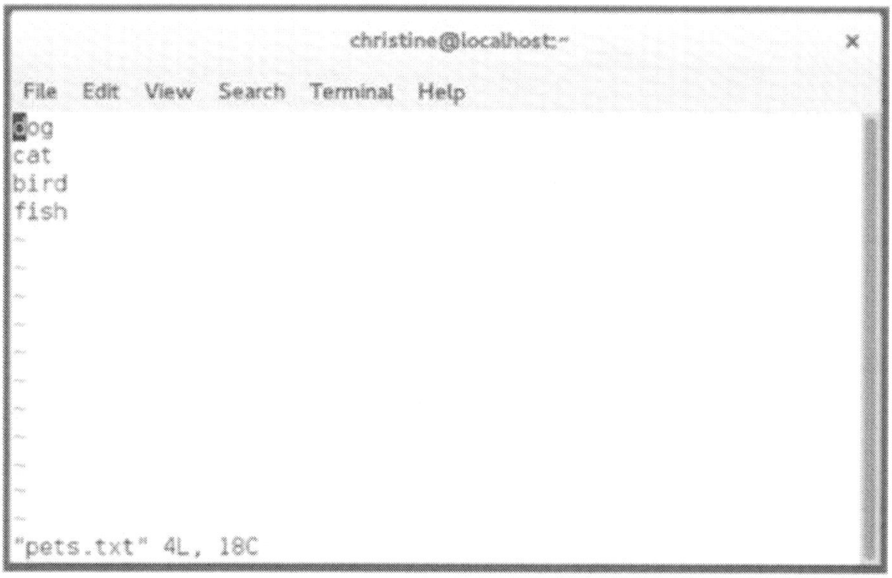

Figure 31: vi text editor

Vi uses keys for commands. Here are some examples:

vi Command	What it does
o	Type this in command mode to insert a new line and enter text
i	Type I to insert succeeding character to the

		left side of the cursor
	u	Undo changes
	ESC	To quit insert mode
	:wq!	To save your changes and quit

Table 12: Sample vi keys

Have you chosen a text editor? Let's now proceed to trying a simple script.

Simple Scripting

A script is a program that can be interpreted by a shell or a compiled program. We call them shell scripts in Linux because most scripts are run in bash or in any other shell (ksh, csh, bash).

Scripts are useful in automating and simplifying administrative tasks, log monitoring of the system, and data processing. To begin scripting, open a text file with vi or a text editor of your choice.

The first line in the file indicates which shell should be used to interpret the script.

```
#!/bin/sh
```

This indicates that the bourne shell should be used to interpret the script.

Let's do a simple script. Enter the following lines of script. Save the file as *simplescript.sh*. Ensure that the file permission for the user is set to 744 so you can run the script as we have learned in chapter 8.

Open a terminal and create a script using your vi editor.

`vi simplescript.sh`

Type i to enter insert mode start entering text. Paste the script below.

```
#!/bin/sh
echo My name is: $1
echo I'm using Linux distro: $2
echo Today is: $3
```

Once done, press on ESC and save the file using the command below.

`:wq!`

Change the file permission:

chmod 744 *simplescript.sh*

Run the script along with 3 arguments:

`./simplescript.sh` *Steve Fedora Tuesday*

The output should be like this:

```
My name is: Steve
I'm using Linux distro: Fedora
Today is: Tuesday
```

Here's an example of how you can use it in maintaining your computer's performance. If you have already used 80% of your disk space, it might be good to check which files are the biggest in your computer.

Write a new script with the command below:

```
find / -type f -atime +30 -size +1000k -exec ls -l {} \; > /tmp/filecleanup
```

This shell script will generate a new file called fileCleanup containing a list of old and big files. As an administrator, the next step is to contact the file owners to give them a notice before deleting these files.

As you might have observed, you can combine different Linux commands with variables, conditional expressions, loops and functions to create your scripts.

At this point, I highly encourage you to proceed in learning advanced Linux where you will learn about more sophisticated and more powerful *awk* and *sed* utilities. These two are especially handy when dealing with data.

Here is a quick recap of what we covered in case you need a refresher on a certain step:

1. You now have an understanding of what Linux is.
2. You now know how Linux compares to other operating systems.
3. You are now familiar with the different Linux distributions and how they differ from each other.
4. You learnt how to prepare for a Linux installation and now have an idea how Linux is installed.
5. You now know the different Linux desktops and their corresponding look and feel.
6. You now have an insight on how a Linux filesystem looks like.
7. You can now navigate in a Linux filesystem.
8. You learnt the basic administration tasks in Linux.
9. You can now create users and restrict access in Linux as part of securing your system.
10. You now have an idea of how scripting works in Linux.

Turn to the next page to gain access to a free video course and to also see my other best-selling books part of this series!

Before You Go

In this book, I have provided you with the basic knowledge that you will need to start your path in learning Linux. The concepts that were initially taught here should help you install Linux on your own computer where you can continue to familiarize yourself with the environment.

I recommend that you learn and take on further topics such as advanced scripting, programming in Linux, and Linux system administration. These added topics would help you gain your Linux Professional certification (if you are eyeing for one). You can also move onto to other programming languages, you can find other popular programming books by visiting our full library at >> http://amzn.to/1Xxmab2

Lastly, continue using and practicing on a Linux computer. Through the knowledge imparted in this book, coupled with practice, you will be able to work on building your Linux career.

You can also join my email list to hear about new content releases as well amongst other cool stuff. As a thank you for joining, you will also receive part one of my popular video course *"25 Website Traffic Methods"* where you will learn different methods to drive targeted traffic to your website or blog. To get access to the course, visit this link >> http://bit.ly/1PtpgK7

Finally, you can also send me an email if you have any questions, feedback or just want to say hello! (I do reply!) My email address is; (Felix_Alvaro@mail.com)

I thank you once again and God bless!

Before You Go, Here Are Other Books Our Readers Loved!

Learn JavaScript Programming Today With This Easy Step-By-Step Guide!

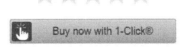

http://amzn.to/1mBhUYM

Learn C Programming Today With This Easy, Step-By-Step Guide

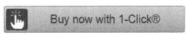

http://amzn.to/1WI6fHu

Learn R Programming With This Easy, Step-By-Step Guide

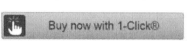

http://amzn.to/24XxoLM

Learn Python Programming Today With This Easy, Step-By-Step Guide!

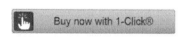

http://amzn.to/1WOBiy2

Learn Java Programming Today With This Easy, Step-By-Step Guide!

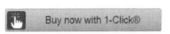

http://amzn.to/1WTgUw0

All You Need To Learn To Drive Tons Of Traffic To Your Website Today!

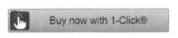

http://amzn.to/21HWFWb

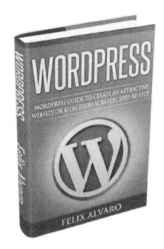 **#1 Best Seller** in Web Site Design

Easily Create Your Own Eye-Catching, Professional Website or Blog Using WordPress Today!

★★★★★

 Buy now with 1-Click®

http://amzn.to/1VHtxZi

GNU
KDE vs Gnome destop
grep
man command